JOHN STAMOS

The Biography

University Press

CONTENTS

PROLOGUE

I t was a reunion that had been long-anticipated –
though the crowd didn't realize it at first.

It was all in the introduction from the late-night
host. Jimmy Fallon, radiating his usual boyish
enthusiasm, knew how to play the hype.

"I'm so excited about our next guest! They're a great
band out of San Francisco. In 1992, their single
Forever became a number one hit – in Japan. And
tonight, they're reuniting for one night only – ladies
and gentlemen, Jesse and the Rippers!"

It had been twenty-five years since John Stamos first
took on the role of Uncle Jesse in *Full House*, and
more than fifteen since the show had wrapped its
final episode. But the crowd that greeted him as he
ran onstage with his bandmates to play under the
giant Smash Club sign was just as enthusiastic about
seeing him as they had been at the height of the
show's popularity. It felt like a time warp, straight
back to 1992 – a feeling only heightened by the fact

that he was dressed in Jesse's clothes, the red shirt, black leather vest, and black leather pants that were undeniable attention-getters. As was the hair – a wig, this time, not his own. He'd looked at himself in the mirror before coming out that night and had to laugh.

Twenty-five years changed a man, there was no doubt about it.

But the more things changed, he reflected, the more they stayed the same.

The songs were the same, and he threw himself into them with the same gusto he'd had since he was a boy, learning to play and entertaining his family. It hadn't ever been just about acting, after all; it was the music. The Beach Boys, the Beatles, Elvis Presley...

No matter what he did, no matter what happened, there was always the music. It was one of the constants in his life.

As he sang his way through the medley, his eyes fell on the familiar figure dancing in the audience, and he grinned. One of the constants, but far from the only one. There was Bob, grooving his heart out, and Lori was in the wings, waiting for her cue.

It was funny, he thought, how the people who had played his family on TV had become such an integral part of his life, even all these years later. It wasn't that he didn't have close family of his own – it was just that there was always room for more.

That, as far as he could tell, was the surest sign of a fortunate man.

Facing the audience that knew every word, John Stamos sang his heart out.

CHAPTER ONE

In a state as crowded as California, in a county as busy as Orange, the little city of Cypress was unusually situated – and unusually lucky. The towns around it were filling up; Los Angeles, less than thirty miles away, already had two and a half million residents. Anaheim, the home of the new Disneyland theme park – not quite ten years old in the early 60s – had over a hundred thousand. But Cypress was small, just about two thousand residents. With small schools, local mom-and-pop shops, and independent cafés, it felt like a little back-country town, even though it was on the threshold of some of the most densely-populated areas in America.

William and Loretta Stamos felt pretty confident that it was the best place to bring up their young family, encouraging them to go after their dreams.

For William – Bill, to everyone who knew him – it was a land of opportunity, just as his father had seen the United States themselves in the same light. Bill's family had come from Greece – with the family name originally being Stamatopolous – establishing themselves in their new country with enthusiasm and an enterprising attitude that was determined to make the best of whatever came their way – an attitude that Bill himself had inherited, and which he would then pass on to his own children. His wife Loretta, meanwhile, was smart, spirited, and beautiful; before their wedding, she had worked as a swimsuit model.

Late in the summer of 1963, they brought their first child home from the hospital.

They named the boy John Philip. From his Greek father, he inherited black hair and dark coloring, with blue eyes standing out in striking contrast. He also inherited his father's wide smile, which appeared regularly. John was a happy-go-lucky, cheerful, funny boy who liked to tell jokes and laugh just as hard at them himself as anyone who was listening.

He also had an artistic side, especially when it came to music. From the time he was little, his parents could see him playing along to the beat of any song he heard. Wanting to stimulate any natural abilities their son might possess, Bill and Loretta bought little John a small drum kit when he was four years old, and encouraged him to make a racket.

The little Stamos family was joined a few years later by two more children – John's younger sisters, Janeen and Alaina. Bill and Loretta worked hard to make the best life possible for their children – Bill, in particular, was something of an entrepreneur, eventually owning three restaurant chains in the local area – but never at the cost of making sure that their children knew how much they were loved. "My mother had enough love to fuel a small country," John would later recall, and his father was his "best friend...They were really good people." Their example while John and his sisters were growing up taught them "to be kind and to be generous and to be loving to everyone that you meet on this journey."

Their early encouragement of John pursuing his interest in music didn't stop when he was in pre-school, either. As he grew older, he expanded his talents, learning to play the keyboard and the guitar, and accompanying himself as he sang the hits he grew up with – he had a special fondness for Elvis. In school, he found friends with similar interests and formed his first band, Destiny, when he was thirteen. The band lasted a little longer than many high school groups do, though not long enough to truly make a mark on the world. Still, it saw John and the other members of the band through their teenage years, earning them paying gigs at parties and local venues.

John and his parents knew that choosing a career in music was no guarantee of success – even though they lived on the edge of the dreamscape of Hollywood, it would take more than the ability to follow a beat to make it. Still, John couldn't help but be attracted to the very idea. From the start, he was a performer – and not just musically, either. From the time he was young, he would entertain his parents, sisters, and friends by putting on magic shows and acting out skits with sock puppets; he cast his sisters and friends to act alongside him and made home movies on his dad's video camera. In school, he recalled, his need for "attention and approval" led to theatrical pranks. "I'd do these makeup jobs with fake blood, and I'd run into the school nurse's office and scream, 'I was hit by a car!'"

In high school, he joined the marching band and played the drums. He enjoyed acting almost as much as he enjoyed music, he found – in junior high, he made his stage debut in the school's production of *Our Town*. Applause, it turned out, was rather addictive.

He didn't just want to be a performer, he decided. He wanted to be a *famous* performer.

Daydreaming of fame was anything but atypical for a teenager, but John put together a checklist of the highs he wanted to hit: he wanted to play with famous musicians, he wanted to have his own sitcom like *Happy Days*, and he wanted to be famous enough not to have to stand in lines at Disneyland, his favorite place on earth. He believed in himself – at the time, though, he was secretly convinced that nobody else thought he could check off any of the things on his list.

Attending John F. Kennedy High in La Palma, he recalls, "I know everybody says this, but in high school, I really was the dorky kid. I was weird... I was into magic and theme parks. I was very innocent. When a lot of kids my age were going out drinking on Friday and Saturday nights, I was at Disneyland, going on the rides and listening to the bands. I didn't think that people liked me...but when I looked back recently at my old yearbooks, people were really nice: 'You're going to make it,' 'See you in Hollywood.' I think I always had it on my radar."

Though Bill and Loretta encouraged John to pursue his dreams, they were too practical to let him get away without putting in the hard work. From the time he was thirteen – about the same time that he was forming his first band with his friends – John went to work at his father's restaurant after school and sometimes on the weekends. Bill had a fast-food place called Yellow Basket; working there, John recalled, was "a part of my childhood." With Bill's go-getter attitude and sense of entrepreneurship, he later branched out and bought "three or four other restaurants," including Orange County-based fast food chains Duke's and Burger Basket. Hard work was far from the only important part of John's childhood – "I lived just eight minutes from Knott's Berry Farm and 20 minutes from Disneyland," he would later reminisce. "I spent my childhood going to those parks, especially Disneyland." But it was an important part of his life, and years later, he would credit his father's work ethic with training his own motivation for success in his career.

"My parents said, 'You want to do it, do it. Just work your ass off, be a good guy, be disciplined.' [My father taught me] discipline for sure. He was like, 'If you're five minutes early, you're 10 minutes late.' Because of my dad and the discipline he had toward his work, I learned to be a pro and arrive early and know my lines and hit my marks." His father's approach to life rubbed off in other ways, too, and John dreamed of being as beloved and respected as his father. "I'll never forget my dad saying, 'When you go to work, don't forget to treat the janitor the same way you treat the producer.' Watching my dad, the way he treated people, stuck with me. He treated the busboy the same way he treated his best customer." That equality and respect, he recalled, was a hallmark of his father's own professional career, as well as his personal life, and it gave John the goal of living up to his parents' standards.

On the whole, the little town of Cypress, California was exactly what Bill and Loretta Stamos had hoped it would be: an ideal place to raise their children to pursue their dreams.

"Orange County helped me to become who I am," John would later express. "I wouldn't be a dreamer if it weren't for where I grew up. I wouldn't have moved forward with an anything-is-possible feeling."

From the early years with his first band to the end of high school, John's dreams kept on growing – and even then, it was just the start of what he would achieve.

CHAPTER TWO

E ven though Bill and Loretta believed it was important to encourage their children to aim for the horizon – John with his dreams of stardom, their two girls both planning to become teachers – they also believed that it was only practical to have a measure of reliability in the future. Bill had worked hard to put together his fast food empire, and all of his children learned discipline in the family business.

"My dad wanted me to go to college to learn business," John reflected much later. "He was grooming me to take over the hamburger joints."

In high school, John's life was full of a stream of classes, work, and playing with his band. The gigs they landed had elevated somewhat over the years. When he was fifteen, he attended his first Beach Boys concert, and fell in love with what he called "heart music – it goes straight to the heart. I had an eight-track of *Endless Summer*, a greatest-hits Beach Boys' album, which I played over and over. When I saw them in concert, I was totally blown away."

In his later teens, he played with a Beach Boys cover band, Papa Doo Run Run, and landed gigs in Disneyland, his favorite place to go. But he knew that, as fun as tribute bands were, they weren't necessarily a solid career choice – and his father knew it too.

The family home wasn't too far away from Cypress College. With encouragement from his father, John decided to bite the bullet and enroll in classes after his graduation. He ran into trouble almost immediately. "I know it sounds stupid, but I was right on the edge of being truly coddled by my mother, and when I started to do things on my own I was a bit lost. I was going to sign up for college, but I couldn't find the sign-up room." John's immediate reaction to this was to abandon the plans for college; after all, he hadn't really wanted to go anyhow. At that point, he had auditioned for a few parts and felt he was getting a handle on what was required to achieve the fame he wanted through acting. His father, although frustrated with his son's lack of drive for his education, agreed that John could skip the first semester and focus on his acting. But the next semester, he warned John, there would be no more excuses. "My dad was like, Next semester you've got to go, and that's that," John recalled. "And I thought – I've got to get on TV!"

Three weeks after his father's ultimatum – and only six months after graduating high school, John auditioned for a role on one of the most famous

– and longest-running – soap operas in America, *General Hospital*.

John wasn't much of a soap opera watcher, but he knew how the formula went. The role was intended to be a guest spot, and wouldn't require much more than a week's worth of work from him; still, the audition process was grueling, covering at least three days, as the competition for the role was hot. John was eighteen years old, with striking features, an engaging smile, and a mischievous look that was ideal for the role of Blackie Parrish, a "bad boy with a heart of gold" archetype from the wrong side of the tracks. He landed the role.

Soap operas are famously nothing if not flexible in their approach to story-telling, and though Blackie was originally written only to be a one-off character, John's acting – and his looks – won the hearts of the powers that be in *General Hospital* production, and he was quickly signed for a two-year contract.

Working on the set was unlike anything John had ever encountered before, and his father's training kicked in. Still, he was determined to have fun with the process – and his focus was still on being famous, which he knew would require a little more than a recurring part on a soap opera. It was a launching pad, but it was hardly the whole trajectory.

"I [still] wanted to be famous," John remembered later, grinning as he recalled the tricks he would play to try to drum up interest in his acting. "We would go to Disneyland or Knott's Berry Farm and [my friend Mike Owen] would run up to me and ask me for my autograph, and everybody was like, 'Who's that?' and I'd sign autographs. Later in life, I was like, 'Oh, wait, this is a craft, I'd better learn, I'd better be good at it.' And I did fall in love with that part of it."

His search for fame was hampered somewhat by the fact that he was still working at the Yellow Basket when he wasn't on set. "I was [acting] during the week, but my dad wouldn't let me quit the restaurant. To my dad, it was about discipline and not knowing how long the acting would last. We didn't realize how big *General Hospital* was. So I would still go to work [at the Yellow Basket] on Sundays and kids were coming to the restaurant for autographs and pictures. And I'm flipping burgers, working the counter, wearing an apron." He laughed. "And I eventually said, 'Dad, I've got to quit. I'm a teen idol.'"

And a teen idol he was indeed. John was named a "certified heartthrob," and not only that, he was good at playing the role he'd been handed. Over the two years that he worked on General Hospital, he earned a Daytime Emmy nomination and won two Soap Opera Digest awards; not bad, considering that his role was only intended to be a one-episode appearance. He also had his first real experiences with romance Hollywood style, dating his co-stars Demi Moore and Janine Turner at different points along the road.

But being a heartthrob, he found, wasn't as easy as he had suspected before it actually happened to him.

The process, he would later state, was "a machine — it's predators and prey and sort of a factory." His bad boy image did him a lot of favors when it came to his development of the character – a trait that he leaned on heavily over the years, as there always seemed to be a demand for those types of characters – but also made him, at least at one point, question where he was heading in life.

Fame, it seemed, was very much a question of which audience you played to.

John's role on *General Hospital* was undoubtedly a hit, but it was far from enough to satisfy his drive to make it big as a breakout star. Not long after taking on the role, he landed another, this time in more of a leading capacity, in the show *Dreams*. The character he played, Gino Minelli, seemed tailored to John: an enterprising, engaging young man trying to get a recording contract with his eponymous band, for which the show was named. Unfortunately, the show didn't have anywhere near the staying power of, for example, General Hospital; twelve episodes were filmed. Seven of them remain unaired to this date. The show was dropped after the first few episodes.

A year or so later, John picked up the role of the

main character's son in the NBC sitcom *You Again?* This one lasted a bit longer, running for two seasons, but it was still far from the starring turn that he was sure he could handle. General Hospital seemed to be the height of his early career – but he was determined not to let it stop there and decided to walk away when his contract ended.

"On *General Hospital*," he recounted, "I had a two-year contract, 30 million people were watching, it became a gigantic thing. I wanted to leave at the end of my deal, and they kept throwing more money at me." On the day he turned twenty, a producer, Gloria Monty, pulled him aside to talk to him privately. "She said, 'Let's go celebrate your birthday, dear.' I knew it wasn't about my birthday."

Sitting in the famous restaurant La Famiglia, at the table next to Dean Martin, Monty leaned across to pinpoint John with her gaze. "So – why do you want to leave now?"

John swallowed nervously. "Well, I want to be funny. I want to be on a sitcom, like *Happy Days*." A visit to the *Happy Days* set on a high school field trip was what had originally got him thinking that acting would be right up his alley; performing, making people laugh, had always been his dream, and he told the producer as much.

Monty leaned back in her chair and eyed him quietly for a minute.

"You know, you'll never work in this town again if you leave the show."

To John, it sounded like a threat. He pictured the restaurant being a "Mafia Italian joint, all the waiters getting the guns out – Gloria hits the floor, Dean hits the floor, and they just take me out..."

But out loud, he managed, "I think I will. I...probably will."

He stuck to his guns and walked away from the soap opera. And for almost a year, he secretly wondered whether he'd made the biggest mistake of his life.

CHAPTER THREE

In 1986, two years after walking away from *General Hospital's* attempts to keep him forever, John was handed a script that he immediately jumped on. The role was the lead in an action film. "*Great!*" he thought. It couldn't be further from the part he'd played in the soap. *This is my shot!* A young James Bond!

But all that glittered, it turned out, was not gold.

The project was a film that looked like a James Bond reboot fueled by late nights and Eighties aesthetics. John's character, the son of a secret agent who had been murdered, takes on the job of avenging his father's death and, along the way, defeating the evil that lurks in the hearts of men. The character's name was Lance Stargrove – a comedically exaggerated caricature of tough-guy leading man nomenclature that seemed out of place in an apparently straightforward action-adventure shoot 'em up. Former Bond actor George Lazenby was brought on to play Lance's father, agent Drew

Stargrove, lending an aura of we-tried-our-best professionalism to the shoot: a Bond, yes, but a *good* Bond? Debatable. Even the name of the film reeked of hand-me-down James Bondism: *Never Too Young To Die*.

At twenty-two years old, though, John missed the red flags. All he saw was the opportunity to take on the lead in his very first film, a sure step up if there ever was one.

The character of Lance Stargrove was a teenage gymnast, giving him a plausible backstory for all sorts of stunt shenanigans throughout the film. Gymnastics was one of the few areas that John had not explored as a teenager, but he did his best to make up for that lack while he prepared for the role, taking gymnastics lessons from a coach – and promptly breaking his ankle. But even a little bodily harm couldn't stop his enthusiasm for the job. "I worked so hard to make it great," he recalled.

The actors that took on the leads alongside John were markedly more experienced, though not necessarily more talented, than John himself. His love interest in the film, Danja Deering, was played by singer Denise Matthews, who already had several years of stardom under her belt under the stage name Vanity. Nearly five years older than John, she had already earned her status as one of the sex symbols of the Eighties, and launched into "seducing" the newcomer as soon as she laid eyes on him. Despite her best efforts, they never ended up as love interests offscreen. "She was kind of a big star," John said. "I was overwhelmed by it all, I guess. I don't want to say anything bad about her because I know she's straightened out her act, but she was pretty wild." Matthews had a tendency to play around with the prop guns that littered the set. "We weren't even rolling, and she was like Al Pacino in *Scarface*, blasting these machine guns all over the place!"

He also found it amusing that Matthews was insistent that her stage name be used at all times, as though it had become her permanent personality. "'Vanity! Call me Vanity!' And I remember telling her, 'Lighten up, Denise!'" A decade later, as a born-again Christian, Matthews would renounce her stage name entirely.

Still, the two got along for the most part. "She was really nice to me. And we did have fun."

The other lead in the film, that of the main villain, went to Gene Simmons of KISS. Even at the time – the mid-Eighties – the role was seen as somewhat problematic, largely because the character was a "murderous psychopathic gang leader" who was also transgender; the writing leaned heavily on the then-common trope of portraying transgender persons as "degenerates." Simmons, as expected, gave it his all; between his performance and decisions made by the makeup and wardrobe department – who also gave it their all, apparently – the result was "scary," according to John. "I guess it was supposed to be like a *Rocky Horror* 'Sweet Transvestite' thing. I think I had nightmares about it because it was Gene's big face with all that makeup and stuff. It was a trip."

When asked about the role, years later, Simmons himself only laughed. "Ah, the folly of youth. That'll teach me to read scripts before accepting roles."

Despite John's enthusiasm for the project – and the sheer audacity of some of the decisions made in development along the way – the film was anything but a hit. It only made a brief appearance in theaters; John had to hunt it down at a nearby drive-in. "I brought a chick," he said ruefully, recalling his hope that his appearance as the lead in the film would impress his date. "Didn't do me any good."

Although it was something of a flop, *Never Too Young To Die* garnered something of a cult following years later. One critic wrote that the film, and especially the performance of Simmons in particular was "insane, but somehow captivating in a way that will cost my therapist thousands of hours of his life," and noted that it was "the kind of film that could only exist in the 80s."

Looking back on it from a much safer vantage point, John commented, "I thought it was going to be the biggest breakthrough. I thought, 'I'm done with TV — I'm going to be a movie star!' And then I did that piece of shit." Still, "I'm at the point in my career where I can look back at things that were really stupid and go, 'Oh my God, I'm so glad I did that!' I can really have a laugh about it, and [*Never Too Young To Die]* is certainly one of the biggest. I would love more people to see it. It's the perfect midnight movie, where people can come and dress up [like for the *Rocky Horror Picture Show*]. It's — what's the term I'm looking for? — the best worst thing you will ever see."

Though it wasn't the career-launching role he'd hoped for, John wasn't about to give up on his dreams of stardom. By this point, in his mid-twenties, he had a few more ego-bolstering experiences to rely on, anyhow – including playing with his favorite band since childhood, the Beach Boys.

Music had always been important to John. From the time he was four years old, he'd poured himself into learning how to create it on any instrument available to him, and playing had always been a significant part of his life plan.

He spent his early childhood, stretching into his teens, listening to eight tracks of his favorite bands on repeat. Orange County was replete with excellent musicians, along with plenty of opportunities to see them play live, and the Stamos family went to concerts regularly in the Cypress area. But it was the Beach Boys concert that John attended in his mid-teens that touched his heart the most – and stuck with him the longest.

As a teenager, every time he would go to a concert, he would find himself daydreaming that someone would come onstage, announce that the drummer had hurt his finger, and ask whether anyone in the audience might be able to fill in. He could see himself so clearly, coming to the rescue, taking his place at the drum kit, wowing the audience, impressing the band, and earning an invitation to come on tour with them, as well as their undying loyalty...

In 1985, a slightly more realistic version of that daydream actually came true when he joined the Beach Boys onstage for his first appearance with the band. It all started when he befriended guitarist Jeffrey Foskett, who played with the Beach Boys in the Eighties; invited to a concert, John was instantly recognized by one of his fellow listeners and the enthusiastic response – most knew him from General Hospital at the time; it's difficult not to wonder whether the response would have been the same if he'd been recognized as the guy from that movie with Gene Simmons in drag – caught the ear of the band. Foskett invited John up on stage, mostly to show his friend off. The crowd went wild.

Foskett, knowing his friend's talent for music, then invited him to sing the next track on the setlist. His time at Disneyland, playing in the Beach Boys cover band, came in handy in a way he had never expected.

"The first song I sang was 'Barbara Ann,'" John

recalled. "I eventually worked my way to the drums. One of the first big shows I did with them was a Fourth of July concert at the Washington Monument. Now they can't get rid of me."

John would continue to play with the band over the next several decades, trading out singing for the drum kit for the guitar and back again – and will undoubtedly continue for the foreseeable future.

"Their music is timeless. I call it heart music, because it goes straight to the heart," he told a reporter, discussing how the music has stuck with him. The older we get, he mused, the more the songs mean: "They're time released. A song like 'Wouldn't It Be Nice' hits harder now and has more emotional impact. [Listening] will make you feel a little better, at least for the night. You're going to leave [any concert] feeling a little more optimistic. That's what happens to me. Without the Beach Boys, life would be a mistake."

Playing with his favorite band would undoubtedly be a major highlight in John's life – but still, it wasn't a stopping point. He was only in his mid-twenties. He had a long way to go before he reached the stardom he'd dreamed of.

And the next step, it turned out, was waiting just around the bend.

CHAPTER FOUR

In the mid-Eighties, Jeff Franklin was looking to move on to the next project in his career path – a path that had only started a few years before, when he served as a writer and producer for Laverne and Shirley and the Tom Hanks sitcom Bosom Bodies. Now, he planned to pitch a new sitcom to ABC. The important part of a situation comedy, in his opinion, was the comedy – he wrote the three male leads as comedians, all living together and pursuing their respective careers to varying degrees of success.

The network didn't turn him down, but they wanted something a little different – namely, a family show. Franklin reworked the premise almost entirely. If they wanted family, he figured, he'd give them family.

The result was the initial set-up for *Full House*. Danny Tanner, the main focus among the three male leads, became a single father of three young daughters after the sudden death of his wife. The second lead, Joey Gladstone, was his childhood best friend. The third was his brother-in-law, who moved into the house to help raise the girls – Uncle Adam Cochran.

ABC ordered a pilot, and Franklin set to casting.

His first choice for Danny was Bob Saget, with Paul Rieser as a close second. Both of them were otherwise occupied at the time, and actor John Posey stepped into the role – later, of course, Bob Saget's contract ended and he happily took on the role of Danny, leading to the pilot being reshot entirely.

Casting Joey was more difficult, as Franklin felt he had created an odd man-child of a character that needed someone who fit the vibe. But once actor Dave Coulier stepped into the room and started reading, it was a shoo-in.

When it came to Uncle Adam Cochran, on the other hand, the process was a little bit different.

"John didn't audition," Franklin recalled. "I set up a lunch with [him]. He was the only name on my list for [the character]. So we went out to lunch and we talked about music — we both loved Elvis, we both loved the Beach Boys. We talked about girls — we made sure we weren't dating the same girl. We just had fun the whole lunch. At the end when the check came, I said, 'We didn't really talk about the show, do you want to do it?' And he's like, 'Oh yeah, I'm in.' That was it. It was that simple. It was the easiest casting process that I've ever been through."

John did have a few requests when it came to the character, though – requests that the writers and producers had no problem acquiescing to. First of all, Adam became Jesse early on. The name just seemed to fit John better. Later, he also requested that Uncle Jesse's last name be changed to something Greek, to reflect his own heritage. It was not the first – nor the last – time that John himself would have an influence on the characters he played. Again, the writers agreed, and Adam Cochran became Uncle Jesse Katsopolis.

Once again, John found himself playing what was essentially the "bad boy with a heart of gold" character. This time, however, he had the time and the freedom to delve into Uncle Jesse and figure out what made him more than just a one-note personality; over the years, Jesse's occasionally obnoxious behavior and womanizing ways were toned down and developed into something more appealing. The camaraderie on set helped a great deal; it took a little while, but by the time the first season was wrapped, John, Bob, Dave, and their other co-stars had already become their own version of a family, just like the characters themselves.

"What's interesting about *Full House* is that it was about three guys—not a mother and a father—who are raising kids," John would later recall. "That was unheard of back then, but now it's the new normal. The thing about [the show] was the kids weren't smartass disrespectful to us, and we weren't disrespectful to them, unlike some shows today that I won't name."

Full House wasn't a hit out of the door, but over the eight seasons of the show, the cast grew closer together, and the love that developed between them echoed the love that the audience felt for the characters. Bob Saget, in particular, became known as America's dad – John, for his part, was known as America's irresponsible Uncle Jesse. Unlike many shows that lasted through a significant run, none of the core cast ever stepped back from beginning to end.

The character of Jesse Katsopolis, though it dovetailed nicely with John's own personal tendencies, evolved over the years as well, going from a notorious flirt who couldn't look at a woman without winking to a married father of two. Jesse's motorcycle-riding, leather-jacket-wearing, Elvis-obsessed genial bad boy seemed tailor-made for John because John himself had a hand in tailoring him. Even his interest in music made an impact on the show; Jesse formed a band, Jesse and the Rippers – interestingly, it read like something of a throwback to John's time on *General Hospital*, where his character's band was called Blackie and the Riff Raff. Even his beloved Beach Boys appeared on the show, in a second season episode called *Beach Boy Bingo.*

Though critics snubbed *Full House* as being saccharine and predictable, there was a wholesome vibe to the show that hit home for many, especially as it became a syndicated staple on television. It was familiar, comfortable in its predictability – exactly what the theme song seems to yearn for – and its audience connected with it on a level that lasted through the next several decades. For John, as for many of the other main cast members, it was a game-changer – the single role with which he is most commonly associated, even now. The show ended in 1995, after a hundred and ninety-two episodes aired, but it seemed to follow them everywhere they went.

"I'm very proud of that show," John would recount much later, "though I haven't watched it in years. It's kind of hard to look at myself in those clothes and with that hair. It looks like I'm wearing a dead crow on my head."

In a way, it was Jesse Katsopolis who gave John Stamos the fame he'd been looking for – and vice versa.

CHAPTER FIVE

In 1994, while John was still playing Uncle Jesse, his personal reputation as a chronic flirt was put to the test when he encountered model Rebecca Romijn backstage at a Victoria's Secret show.

Sparks flew between the two immediately. Within a few months, they were rumored to be an item, but it took four years before John asked her to marry him – Christmas Eve, 1997. She gladly said yes, and in September 1998, they said their I do's at the Beverly Hills Hotel. John's *Full House* castmates all attended; Candace Cameron Bure remembers him crying on his wedding day.

Rebecca, John told a reporter, posed a challenge for him, one that he appreciated: "When I'm around her I want to be a better person."

Rebecca, following a rare trend among Hollywood starlets, immediately grafted her married name onto her professional moniker, being credited as Rebecca Romijn-Stamos in *X-Men*, *Austin Powers*, and *The Punisher*, among others. While her star was undeniably rising, John's own fame seemed to be entering something of a lull. Followed everywhere by the ghost of Uncle Jesse, he turned to a series of starkly different roles – murders, criminals, all-around bad guys, just to try and distance himself from *Full House*. He still felt a fondness for Uncle Jesse, and never let up on his close relationship with his erstwhile castmates; still, the last thing he wanted was to be pigeonholed forever into the type of role he'd started out with. He returned his attention more to his music, too – and in 2000, he was finally able to work on a project involving the Beach Boys, which he had been planning for years; he produced a mini-series about the band, *The Beach Boys: An American Family*. "I'm always trying to get a younger generation to learn about the Beach Boys!"

He also returned to TV in the lead role in a show called *Thieves*, a premise that took two thieves and turned them into government agents in order to avoid serving time for their own crimes, along the lines of *White Collar*; the show aired several episodes and generated a lot of excitement, but ultimately was canceled before the end of the first season.

In the meantime, while in the honeymoon phase of his marriage, being a good husband seemed easy. The two were like children, playing house. "Most of the time I'm tackling her in the backyard and tickling her, or we turn on music and practice weird dance steps," John told a reporter at the time, when asked what he and Rebecca did for fun.

"We chase each other around the house like goofballs," Rebecca put in. "He just makes me laugh so hard, my sides ache."

On one particular occasion – John's thirty-sixth birthday – the couple threw a cross-dressing-themed party for their friends. Rebecca dressed up as John "in the Eighties – with a really bad wig," and John himself dressed up as a French maid. "I think I was the ugliest woman I've ever seen."

Despite the strength of the connection between them, and the fact that they generally got along very well, John and Rebecca's marriage began to derail after the first few years. It was made more difficult to keep up appearances when John's father – whom he had called his best friend – passed away.

Bill Stamos had been a rock for all three of his children, and unlike many who made it big in Hollywood, John had never forgotten his roots. It was his father's encouragement that had pushed him to give acting a serious try; it was his father's training that had kept him at work, showing up on time, disciplined, and dedicated. Suddenly, with Bill gone, it was as though John's life was turned upside down.

His relationship with Rebecca quickly became more rocky than ever. Playing house with your best friend was fun for a while, but for two grown adults, it was an untenable position – there was also the question of where their lives together were headed. Both of them wanted kids, but with Rebecca's career at such a high point, they could not agree on when to start their family.

By the time John accompanied Rebecca to the premiere of *X-Men 2* in 2003, the two had already been split up for months, though they would not announce it officially until 2004. John filed for divorce, citing irreconcilable differences, and their marriage was brought to an end after just over five years.

John's life, already somewhat unsteady, hit an undeniably rough patch. He had dreamed of being a good husband and a father – suddenly, it all seemed to be slipping away. His career, too, was beginning to wander; for years, he had tried to distance himself from Uncle Jesse, but the end result was that he found himself in a directionless mix of roles, none of which seemed to build on what had come before. Deciding to return to the world of sitcoms, he took on the role of Jake, a New York City publicist with familiarly womanizing tendencies who – also familiarly – looks for the woman of his dreams, as only she can change him for the better. The show *Jake In Progress* was initially set up to be a real-time portrayal of Jake's attempts at dating; the concept was abandoned, though the premise remained, and then the show was abandoned – twice. After the first season, it was canceled, then picked up again, and then promptly canceled again after one more episode aired.

Over the next several years, John would find one-off and cameo roles in big shows – in an episode of *Friends*, he played a hapless fellow who is interviewed as a sperm donor by Chandler and Monica; he appeared in two episodes of *ER*, eventually being added as a series regular. In 2010 he was added to the cast of Glee, as the dentist love interest of Emma Pillsbury; in the previous season, the writers of Glee had made John the butt of a joke, with Emma herself remarking, "They say it takes more certainty than talent to be a star. I mean, look at John Stamos."

At the time, the comment had gotten under John's skin; "I was pissed," he told reporters, and even called the head of Fox TV programming to complain about the jab.

Brad Falchuk, one of Glee's producers, apologized for the incident and explained that the comment never would have been made except for the type of persona that John exuded. "We needed someone iconic to use in that joke, and John seemed like the perfect mix of a guy who could take it. It's surprising when you talk to him. He's vulnerable without being neurotic. He's very endearing.

"I'm not the guy who bursts into the room," John would later admit. "I'm the most insecure person you'll meet if you get to know me."

Whether the offer of a recurring role on the show was meant as an olive branch or it was simply because John was perfect for the part is up for debate, but whatever the case, John didn't let his hurt feelings stop him from taking Falchuk up on the chance.

In between TV roles, John returned to the stage again. He'd previously made his first appearance on Broadway in 1997, in *How to Succeed in Show Business Without Really Trying*; he'd also appeared in *Cabaret* and *NINE,* among others. "I work all the time," he told an interviewer around this time. "Sometimes it's a super high profile show like *ER* or *Glee*, or a Super Bowl commercial." He'd also taken on the role of the face of Dannon's Greek yogurt brand, Oikos; the first Super Bowl ad spot featured him teasing a woman by refusing to share spoonfuls of the yogurt, leading to her abruptly head-butting him in the face and stealing it for herself. "And then I'll kind of go quiet, which means I'm working in theater or I'm producing. A year and a half ago, I was with James Earl Jones and Angela Lansbury in *The Best Man*, and nobody talked about it. All people want to talk about is *Full House*."

In 2009, John appeared in the Broadway revival of *Bye Bye Birdie*. Broadway, again, presented an entirely different set of challenges than either film or TV, but the chance to sing for his supper – quite literally – was not something that John ever passed up. The role earned him a Golden Icon Award for best actor in a musical.

Later that year, he achieved another first – a brilliantly bright spot in a difficult time in his life – when he was given his own star on the Hollywood Walk of Fame.

But despite the bright spots, it was clear that things were not going as well as he had dreamed they would. The biggest check to his trajectory occurred in 2014, when his mother, Loretta, passed away. As he had with his father, John had kept a close relationship with his mom – after Bill died, that bond was stronger than ever, in what John called a "healthy codependent relationship."

"My mom and I became very, very close. I got a divorce pretty close to my dad dying, and we both had gigantic holes in our hearts and our souls. My dad was the only man she ever loved. She lived in Orange County, and I would go down almost every weekend and stay with her. She called it the Castle of Comfort. It got to a point where it might have been hampering me from meeting someone, 'cause when I was lonely, I was depressed, I was upset, I'd just go down to my mother's house, which is where I grew up, and be surrounded by that love which was always there, and all the old stuff. She kept everything down to my tonsils."

Having lost both of his parents, the guiding lights throughout his life, and with the Castle of Comfort empty and barren, he felt more lost than ever. "A piece of me just was gone. It was a big part of my purpose for many, many years to be there for her and be a good son."

Like many in Hollywood, John had turned to alcohol and other avenues to numb any pain, celebrate his triumphs, and generally help him to cope. After the loss of both parents, on top of the dissolution of his marriage to Rebecca and the strain of juggling so many roles in his professional life, the urge to dull his pain grew stronger than ever.

Throughout his career, he told Howard Stern in an interview, he "could stop drinking on a dime," whenever it was necessary. But in the midst of all the stresses and tragedies, his drinking got the better of him, and in 2015, he was arrested under a DUI charge – for which he was convicted and sentenced to three years of probation.

Each time he went back to drinking over the years, he told Stern, "it just sort of deteriorated my life, and who I was, and my morals and my values. I lost myself, I lost my sense of discipline, which my dad taught me so well, and I just became someone [else] – more and more I was just dipping into that dark place. It happened more and more. It just got darker and darker, and it stunted my growth. I remember, too, around that time, looking in a mirror and going, 'Who have I turned into? I'm not the person my parents raised.'" The DUI, he said, was "horrific – I am so embarrassed by [it.] I could have hurt somebody. It was really stupid and ignorant of me. And I hated myself for that. It was a bad, bad thing. So I said to myself, I have to stop this up and down, up and down. I *have* to."

The answer, he knew, was to check himself into rehab, and he did so immediately, going into a residential facility for thirty days.

"I walked in those doors, I said, 'Tell me what to do. I'll do anything I can. I'm going to apply myself a hundred percent to it.'" This promise, he admitted, was something he'd never really done over the years, even in the times he had tried to stop drinking. This time, though, was different – he had lost his parents, true, but he knew only too well how Bill and Loretta would react to hearing that their son had come so close to disaster.

His parents had done their best to raise him right – to be kind, to be generous, to be loving to everyone he met.

He was determined, now more than ever, that he was going to make them proud.

CHAPTER SIX

Over the years, John had a decidedly up-and-down relationship with the ghost of himself, who went by the name "Uncle Jesse." After the success of Full House, it seemed that it was impossible to go anywhere without being recognized as America's irresponsible uncle; for years, he fought against it, certain that he could make his mark as something else, something better. As the decades went by, though, he started to rethink the whole thing. Uncle Jesse – and the family that was associated with him – had been good to John. If it weren't for that role in Full House, he wouldn't have so many of the important people who still had regular appearances in the sitcom of his life – especially Bob Saget, who had become the brother he'd always wanted.

When the prospect of a *Full House* revival came around, he decided he was fully on board.

It wasn't the first time that the idea had been suggested, and over the years, the project had taken on many forms. John had an ownership stake in the show, and lent his energies and enthusiasm to bringing the old magic back. In the end, it was structured as a sequel, to be called *Fuller House* – none of the production team were inclined to mess with success, and so the set-up of the show was markedly similar to the original sitcom. This time around, Danny's daughter DJ was the lead, as a recently widowed mother of three. Her sister Stephanie and best friend Kimmy joined her to help raise her boys; the group moved into the Tanner family home, keeping the surroundings comfortably familiar – and profitably nostalgic for fans of the original show.

John stepped back into the role of Uncle Jesse with almost unbelievable ease – though that ease was facilitated by the fact that, more so than any of his co-stars, he appeared to be more or less untouched by the passage of time. "John Stamos looks the same as he looked on *Full House* - How is that even possible?" wondered one writer. The notable exception is the mullet, fortunately – or unfortunately, for business-in-the-front, party-in-the-back fans.

The vibe of the show, along with the return of most of the main cast, hit right at the heart of fans of the original, many of whom introduced their children to *Full House* after watching the sequel with their families. In the end, it ran for five seasons.

The chance to get to act once more with his old

friends brought a renewed light and energy to John's life – not to mention his career. Over the years, he'd appeared with his former castmates in other projects, such as Bob Saget's parody film *Farce of the Penguins* – he'd also been the roastmaster for Bob's Comedy Central Roast, and there had been *Full House* mini-reunions along the way, such as when they appeared two separate times on Jimmy Fallon's show. But the episodes of *Fuller House* that they did together were special, a time warp to the past.

And a few years later, when John heard the shocking news that Bob had suddenly passed away, that time became even more treasured.

Bob Saget was only sixty-five years old when he was found dead in his hotel room; he had been on tour, delivering a stand-up show mere hours before his death. John, who had stayed closer to Bob than to the others in the cast, though he loved them all, was one of the first to react.

"I am broken. I am gutted," he wrote. "I am in complete and utter shock.

I will never ever have another friend like him. I love you so much, Bobby."

The news took Bob's family, friends, and fans aback by its suddenness. Only a few hours before, Bob had posted about how his shows were going, expressing his gratitude for where he had gotten to in his life.

"When I saw his last Instagram post, my first

thought was he looked too alive to die a few hours later. He died bright and fierce," John would later say. "But... I guess that's right. We should all want to 'die alive.' We don't want to be filled with regret and remorse, forgotten and discarded. We want to be overwhelmed with the privilege...of doing what we do best."

John's tribute to his friend came from the heart – and it was a comfort to know that Bob felt the same way about him. Just a few years before his death, Bob had posted a congratulatory birthday message for John: *"To say we are like brothers is an understatement...but what I have to say here is how damned lucky I am to have John in my life. He has always been there for me. Even when I could be unbearable. Anyone who knows him knows what a beautiful person he is. And I'm not talkin' about his gift of looks. I'm talkin' about the gift of his heart. I've learned so much from John, and I am truly blessed to have this good man as my brother. There is only one John Stamos on this planet, and I am a better person because he's in my life."*

In the late Eighties, John had become part of a fictional family in *Full House* – a fictional family that had grown together, tightly-knit, as real as any blood ties. When he, along with everyone else, lost America's dad, that was how he mourned, too – as part of a family.

CHAPTER SEVEN

In 2018, John reached a milestone that he had started to worry he never would – he became a father.

He'd met and married model Caitlin McHugh after dating her for just a year. Their first date, he recounted, was at Disney World – Disney still being his favorite place on earth.

"We were in Epcot, and I had a hat and glasses, walking around. I was like, 'Nobody's recognizing me. I've got to impress this girl with my fame.' So I take my glasses off and try to make eye contact with people, like a weirdo. Then I take my hat off — I have famous hair. I'm, like, doing catchphrases. 'Have mercy!' And she said, 'What are you doing?' I said, 'Oh, nothing.' She said, 'You're trying to get recognized, aren't you?' I said, 'No, why would I do that?'" Telling the story, he can't help but laugh. "So now the term is 'Epcotting,' if she ever catches me trying to get recognized."

At least, he might have pointed out, he didn't have his old friend Mike Owen run up and ask for his autograph, as he had done back in the General Hospital days.

Regardless of his Epcotting, when he asked Caitlin to marry him, she quickly said yes. They married in February 2018, and their son was born in April that same year.

In honor of his father, they named him Billy.

Being a parent – like every new thing he'd ever tried in his life – brought with it a whole new flock of challenges. Still, John readily acknowledged that he hadn't been "mature enough" to handle being a father earlier in his life, though he had wanted kids his whole life. "I figured, 'I can't wait to be a father.' I've been a TV father, but it's a whole different ballgame. It's the greatest blessing of my life. I couldn't imagine my life without him – but it is challenging to do it right. It just takes so much to be a good parent – it's about sacrifice, it's an enormous amount of love, an enormous amount of patience, common sense, teaching them values and what's right and wrong... and everything's expensive..."

His role as America's favorite irresponsible uncle had finally been outgrown, it seemed. He wasn't quite ready to step into Bob's shoes as America's dad, but being Billy Stamos's dad – that, he could handle.

John's affection for children and desire to have kids

of his own had been a part of his life since he was hardly more than a kid himself. Though it wasn't until his late fifties that the dream became real, he could look back on his life and know that he had done what he could for other kids – in 2005, he'd started to serve as the national spokesman for Project Cuddle, a nonprofit organization dedicated to preventing the abandonment of children by working with pregnant women and adoptive families. The same month that Billy was born, John and Caitlin announced the formation of a jewelry line, St. Amos Jewelry, with their entire portion of the profits to be donated to Childhelp, a charitable foundation focused on helping victims of child abuse.

And now, with a child of his own, he was determined to continue the cycle by doing his best to raise his son as his parents had raised him: to be conscientious, hard-working, disciplined, and to be kind, generous, and loving to everyone he met.

Being a father, he told a reporter recently, "means that I don't have to hand a kid back to the parents when someone yells 'Cut!' It means when people ask me if I'm a father, I don't have to use the goofy line, 'No, but I play one on TV.' [It] means that from this day forward— I will start to look my age...and older. I'm telling you, one day, I'm not going to look so good, so I'm going to start prepping people for that. Most importantly, it means that for the rest of my life, I'll always be known as someone's dad. And that's all I ever wanted."

Bill Stamos, John recounted, "was the greatest superhero to me. He never became human. He was always the coolest guy. He was always bigger than life to me. Now, the universe is saying to me, 'It's your turn.'"

Newly sixty years old, John might find it easy to feel that he still has a long way to go to check everything off the list he made when he was a teenager. But the important things, the things that matter the most in life, have all been handled. "I went into becoming an adult kicking and screaming...[but now] I am so grateful that I'm settled, and I'm cool, and I'm sober, and I'm happy with myself."

Music career: check.

Acting fame: check.

A sitcom like *Happy Days*: check.

Skipping the rides at Disneyland: check. ("They accommodate me.")

Following in the footsteps of his loving parents as he launches himself into the biggest and most important role of his life, fatherhood: check, check, check.

If John Stamos still has a long way to go and a lot to do, one thing is evident – he's going to enjoy every minute of it.

Made in the USA
Middletown, DE
17 December 2023